MAD LIBS®

GAME OVER! MAD LIBS

by Brandon T. Snider

Mad Libs
An Imprint of Penguin Rando

MAD LIBS
Penguin Young Readers Group
An Imprint of Penguin Random House LLC

Concept created by Roger Price & Leonard Stern

Published by Mad Libs,
an imprint of Penguin Random House LLC,
345 Hudson Street, New York, New York 10014.
Printed in the USA.

ISBN 9780843183696

19 20 18

MAD LIBS® INSTRUCTIONS

MAD LIBS® is a game for people who don't like games! It can be played by one, two, three, four, or forty.

• RIDICULOUSLY SIMPLE DIRECTIONS

In this tablet you will find stories containing blank spaces where words are left out. One player, the READER, selects one of these stories. The READER does not tell anyone what the story is about. Instead, he/she asks the other players, the WRITERS, to give him/her words. These words are used to fill in the blank spaces in the story.

• TO PLAY

The READER asks each WRITER in turn to call out a word—an adjective or a noun or whatever the space calls for—and uses them to fill in the blank spaces in the story. The result is a MAD LIBS® game.

When the READER then reads the completed MAD LIBS® game to the other players, they will discover that they have written a story that is fantastic, screamingly funny, shocking, silly, crazy, or just plain dumb—depending upon which words each WRITER called out.

• EXAMPLE (*Before* and *After*)

"________________ !" he said ________________
EXCLAMATION ADVERB

as he jumped into his convertible ________________ and
NOUN

drove off with his ________________ wife.
ADJECTIVE

" *Ouch* !" he said *stupidly*
EXCLAMATION ADVERB

as he jumped into his convertible *cat* and
NOUN

drove off with his *brave* wife.
ADJECTIVE

MAD LIBS QUICK REVIEW

In case you have forgotten what adjectives, adverbs, nouns, and verbs are, here is a quick review:

An ADJECTIVE describes something or somebody. *Lumpy*, *soft*, *ugly*, *messy*, and *short* are adjectives.

An ADVERB tells how something is done. It modifies a verb and usually ends in "ly." *Modestly*, *stupidly*, *greedily*, and *carefully* are adverbs.

A NOUN is the name of a person, place, or thing. *Sidewalk*, *umbrella*, *bridle*, *bathtub*, and *nose* are nouns.

A VERB is an action word. *Run*, *pitch*, *jump*, and *swim* are verbs. Put the verbs in past tense if the directions say PAST TENSE. *Ran*, *pitched*, *jumped*, and *swam* are verbs in the past tense.

When we ask for A PLACE, we mean any sort of place: a country or city (*Spain*, *Cleveland*) or a room (*bathroom*, *kitchen*).

An EXCLAMATION or SILLY WORD is any sort of funny sound, gasp, grunt, or outcry, like *Wow!*, *Ouch!*, *Whomp!*, *Ick!*, and *Gadzooks!*

When we ask for specific words, like a NUMBER, a COLOR, an ANIMAL, or a PART OF THE BODY, we mean a word that is one of those things, like *seven*, *blue*, *horse*, or *head*.

When we ask for a PLURAL, it means more than one. For example, *cat* pluralized is *cats*.

MAD LIBS® is fun to play with friends, but you can also play it by yourself! To begin with, DO NOT look at the story on the page below. Fill in the blanks on this page with the words called for. Then, using the words you have selected, fill in the blank spaces in the story.

Now you've created your own hilarious MAD LIBS® game!

PREPARE TO FIGHT!

ADJECTIVE ______________________

VERB ENDING IN "ING" ______________________

TYPE OF FOOD ______________________

NOUN ______________________

VERB ______________________

NUMBER ______________________

VERB ______________________

PART OF THE BODY (PLURAL) ______________________

VERB ______________________

TYPE OF FOOD ______________________

PLURAL NOUN ______________________

ADJECTIVE ______________________

ADJECTIVE ______________________

NOUN ______________________

NOUN ______________________

NOUN ______________________

VERB ______________________

MAD LIBS®

PREPARE TO FIGHT!

Mario: What a/an ____________ day, eh Luigi? The perfect day for
ADJECTIVE

__________________ some Koopas. The ____________ Kingdom is
VERB ENDING IN "ING" — TYPE OF FOOD

crawling with them!

Luigi: You're right about that, dear ____________. I hope you're ready
NOUN

to ____________.
VERB

Mario: Ready? I've waited __________ years to ____________ that
NUMBER — VERB

scoundrel Bowser!

Luigi: Pipe down. He has ____________________ everywhere.
PART OF THE BODY (PLURAL)

Mario: First, I'll ____________ and grab a/an ____________. That'll
VERB — TYPE OF FOOD

give me ______________.
PLURAL NOUN

Luigi: And I'll grab a/an ____________ star. Then I'll be the most
ADJECTIVE

____________ plumber of all time.
ADJECTIVE

Mario: Remember we're there to rescue Princess ____________, Luigi.
NOUN

Once we do that we'll be heroes!

Luigi: Then let's slide down that pipe and save the ____________!
NOUN

Mario: That's the spirit, brother! Get your ____________ ready. It's
NOUN

time to ____________!
VERB

MAD LIBS® is fun to play with friends, but you can also play it by yourself! To begin with, DO NOT look at the story on the page below. Fill in the blanks on this page with the words called for. Then, using the words you have selected, fill in the blank spaces in the story.

Now you've created your own hilarious MAD LIBS® game!

A LEGEND

NUMBER ______

ADJECTIVE ______

NOUN ______

COLOR ______

NOUN ______

VERB ENDING IN "ING" ______

ADJECTIVE ______

NOUN ______

ADJECTIVE ______

ADJECTIVE ______

FIRST NAME (FEMALE) ______

NOUN ______

ADJECTIVE ______

PLURAL NOUN ______

VERB ______

ADJECTIVE ______

PLURAL NOUN ______

VERB ______

MAD LIBS®

A LEGEND

Hidden within the Kingdom of Hyrule are __________ (NUMBER) pieces of a/an __________ (ADJECTIVE) __________ (NOUN) known as the Triforce. This __________ (COLOR) __________ (NOUN) holds the key to defeating the evil warlord Ganon and __________ (VERB ENDING IN "ING") Princess Zelda. Only the heroic Link can save the day! He must use his __________ (ADJECTIVE) __________ (NOUN) to defeat __________ (ADJECTIVE) monsters and battle dark forces throughout the kingdom. Link will have to fight his way through the __________ (ADJECTIVE) Woods, Lake __________ (FIRST NAME (FEMALE)) and the famous Death __________ (NOUN)! But first he'll need to find the __________ (ADJECTIVE) Sword. Join Link as he collects __________ (PLURAL NOUN) that will help him __________ (VERB) his enemies. Help him as he discovers __________ (ADJECTIVE) dungeons and explores lost __________ (PLURAL NOUN). Will he be able to __________ (VERB) the Princess in time? You decide!

MAD LIBS® is fun to play with friends, but you can also play it by yourself! To begin with, DO NOT look at the story on the page below. Fill in the blanks on this page with the words called for. Then, using the words you have selected, fill in the blank spaces in the story.

Now you've created your own hilarious MAD LIBS® game!

GAMER GEAR MUST-HAVES!

ADJECTIVE ________________

NOUN ________________

A PLACE ________________

ANIMAL ________________

NUMBER ________________

PLURAL NOUN ________________

ADJECTIVE ________________

NOUN ________________

VERB ________________

A PLACE ________________

TYPE OF LIQUID ________________

NOUN ________________

VERB ________________

ADJECTIVE ________________

VERB ENDING IN "ING" ________________

NUMBER ________________

NOUN ________________

MAD LIBS®

GAMER GEAR MUST-HAVES!

What does a gamer need in order to ensure ultimate victory?

- **Sound 'Splosion:** This ____________ (ADJECTIVE) headset brings the ____________ (NOUN) straight to your ____________ (A PLACE)! With sound so clear, you'll feel like a/an ____________ (ANIMAL) tracking its prey.
- **Crunch Trough:** After a long day of battling evil, you definitely need some snacks. How about ____________ (NUMBER) different varieties including Potato ____________ (PLURAL NOUN), Choco Bites, and ____________ (ADJECTIVE) Frosted Mini Biscuits. Yum!
- **Vermintech:** This cordless ____________ (NOUN) allows you to ____________ (VERB) without any hassle. It's so good you can even use it in (the) ____________ (A PLACE).
- **Doozie Coozie:** Are you tired of your ____________ (TYPE OF LIQUID) spilling all over your ____________ (NOUN)? Your drink will never ____________ (VERB) again with this ____________ (ADJECTIVE) holder.
- **Isolator 5000:** The ultimate ____________ (VERB ENDING IN "ING") console is here! ____________ (NUMBER) games at your disposal! You won't want to leave your ____________ (NOUN)-room ever again!

MAD LIBS® is fun to play with friends, but you can also play it by yourself! To begin with, DO NOT look at the story on the page below. Fill in the blanks on this page with the words called for. Then, using the words you have selected, fill in the blank spaces in the story.

Now you've created your own hilarious MAD LIBS® game!

BUILD A WORLD FROM SCRATCH

NOUN ____________________

COLOR ____________________

ADJECTIVE ____________________

NOUN ____________________

OCCUPATION ____________________

VERB ____________________

OCCUPATION ____________________

PLURAL NOUN ____________________

ADJECTIVE ____________________

ADVERB ____________________

PLURAL NOUN ____________________

VERB ____________________

ADVERB ____________________

NUMBER ____________________

ANIMAL (PLURAL) ____________________

ADJECTIVE ____________________

NOUN ____________________

VERB ____________________

MAD LIBS®

BUILD A WORLD FROM SCRATCH

Step 1: Welcome to Peepsylvania! Choose a/an ____________ (NOUN) for your Peep. It can be anything you want. It can even be ____________ (COLOR). Just make sure it looks ____________ (ADJECTIVE). Remember, a Peep is a regular ____________ (NOUN) just like you and me.

Step 2: Log in and begin! Your Peep needs a job. Is it a/an ____________ (OCCUPATION)? Does it ____________ (VERB) all day long? Or it could be a/an ____________ (OCCUPATION) instead. Then it would collect ____________ (PLURAL NOUN), but only if they're ____________ (ADJECTIVE). Choose ____________ (ADVERB)!

Step 3: Now it's time to make the ____________ (PLURAL NOUN). If you ____________ (VERB) them, make sure you do it ____________ (ADVERB). Once you've assembled ____________ (NUMBER) ____________ (ANIMAL (PLURAL)), you're ready to start. Good luck!

Step 4: You've reached the ____________ (ADJECTIVE) level. Now your Peep is a Royal ____________ (NOUN). This allows it to ____________ (VERB) over all the other Peeps in Peepsylvania. Congratulations!

MAD LIBS® is fun to play with friends, but you can also play it by yourself! To begin with, DO NOT look at the story on the page below. Fill in the blanks on this page with the words called for. Then, using the words you have selected, fill in the blank spaces in the story.

Now you've created your own hilarious MAD LIBS® game!

WELCOME!

ADJECTIVE ____________________

PLURAL NOUN ____________________

OCCUPATION (PLURAL) ____________________

ADJECTIVE ____________________

NOUN ____________________

ADJECTIVE ____________________

VERB ____________________

VERB ____________________

VERB ____________________

NOUN ____________________

PERSON IN ROOM ____________________

A PLACE ____________________

A PLACE ____________________

CITY ____________________

NUMBER ____________________

VERB ____________________

PART OF THE BODY ____________________

MAD LIBS®

WELCOME!

Welcome to Skylands, a/an ____________ (ADJECTIVE) kingdom high above the ____________ (PLURAL NOUN). It's here where a group of ____________ (OCCUPATION (PLURAL)) use their abilities to combat the ____________ (ADJECTIVE) forces of Kaos, an evil ____________ (NOUN). The ____________ (ADJECTIVE) Skylanders ____________ (VERB) against Kaos using the power of the Elements. Blast Zone can ____________ (VERB) with the power of Fire, and Wash Buckler can ____________ (VERB) with the power of Water. For centuries, the Skylanders protected the ____________ (NOUN) of Light with the help of their mentors, the Portal Masters. One such mentor, known as ____________ (PERSON IN ROOM), gathered heroes from (the) ____________ (A PLACE), (the) ____________ (A PLACE), and ____________ (CITY). Soon there were over ____________ (NUMBER) Skylanders ready to join the battle. Together they ____________ (VERB) for what's right, even in the ____________ (PART OF THE BODY) of great danger.

MAD LIBS® is fun to play with friends, but you can also play it by yourself! To begin with, DO NOT look at the story on the page below. Fill in the blanks on this page with the words called for. Then, using the words you have selected, fill in the blank spaces in the story.

Now you've created your own hilarious MAD LIBS® game!

AN INSANE ASYLUM

ADJECTIVE ____________________

TYPE OF FOOD ____________________

ADJECTIVE ____________________

ADJECTIVE ____________________

VERB ____________________

ARTICLE OF CLOTHING ____________________

ADJECTIVE ____________________

NUMBER ____________________

PLURAL NOUN ____________________

NOUN ____________________

VERB ____________________

NOUN ____________________

VERB ____________________

ADJECTIVE ____________________

A PLACE ____________________

VERB ____________________

VERB ____________________

MAD LIBS®

AN INSANE ASYLUM

Arkham Asylum is a/an ____________ (ADJECTIVE) place. It's covered in darkness and smells like old ____________ (TYPE OF FOOD). Is it the most ____________ (ADJECTIVE) place in Gotham City? Probably. And I'm trapped here with all the ____________ (ADJECTIVE) inmates. My worst enemies have come together to ____________ (VERB) against me. It's a good thing I've got my utility ____________ (ARTICLE OF CLOTHING). It's got everything I need including a/an ____________ (ADJECTIVE) Laser, ____________ (NUMBER) ____________ (PLURAL NOUN), and a/an ____________ (NOUN) that can ____________ (VERB). I don't know if that will be enough to stop the Clown ____________ (NOUN) of Crime. The Joker continues to ____________ (VERB) Gotham with his ____________ (ADJECTIVE) capers. Now he's taken control of Arkham's ____________ (A PLACE) and wants to ____________ (VERB) it up. I've got to take him out in order to ____________ (VERB) the city. I'll show him what justice is all about. No one can hide from Batman!

MAD LIBS® is fun to play with friends, but you can also play it by yourself! To begin with, DO NOT look at the story on the page below. Fill in the blanks on this page with the words called for. Then, using the words you have selected, fill in the blank spaces in the story.

Now you've created your own hilarious MAD LIBS® game!

PEPPERMINT CRUSH

FIRST NAME (FEMALE) ____________________

NOUN ____________________

ADJECTIVE ____________________

VERB ENDING IN "ING" ____________________

PERSON IN ROOM ____________________

VERB ENDING IN "ING" ____________________

NUMBER ____________________

A PLACE ____________________

ADJECTIVE ____________________

PLURAL NOUN ____________________

COLOR ____________________

VERB ____________________

COLOR ____________________

VERB ENDING IN "ING" ____________________

OCCUPATION ____________________

ADJECTIVE ____________________

NOUN ____________________

TYPE OF FOOD (PLURAL) ____________________

MAD LIBS®

PEPPERMINT CRUSH

Mom: ________________ (FIRST NAME (FEMALE)), can you show me how to play *Peppermint Crush*? I just downloaded it onto my new ____________ (NOUN). It looks ____________ (ADJECTIVE). So many colors. How fun!

Daughter: Mom, I can't right now. I'm busy ________________ (VERB ENDING IN "ING"). Can't you ask ____________ (PERSON IN ROOM)?

Mom: I'm not ________________ (VERB ENDING IN "ING") too much here. It'll only take __________ (NUMBER) minutes. Please? It will give me something to do when I'm at (the) ____________ (A PLACE).

Daughter: Fine! Whatever. It's ____________ (ADJECTIVE). You just move the ______________ (PLURAL NOUN) together. They have to be the same color.

Mom: What about the ____________ (COLOR) ones? Can I ____________ (VERB) those with the ____________ (COLOR) ones?

Daughter: No! Are you even ________________ (VERB ENDING IN "ING")?

Mom: Do not yell at me, please. I'm not a/an ______________ (OCCUPATION), and I'm not some ____________ (ADJECTIVE) ____________ (NOUN). I am your mother. Now help me collect more ________________ (TYPE OF FOOD (PLURAL)). I love you.

MAD LIBS® is fun to play with friends, but you can also play it by yourself! To begin with, DO NOT look at the story on the page below. Fill in the blanks on this page with the words called for. Then, using the words you have selected, fill in the blank spaces in the story.

Now you've created your own hilarious MAD LIBS® game!

ONE MORE GAME

NOUN ____________________

ADJECTIVE ____________________

ADJECTIVE ____________________

PART OF THE BODY ____________________

VERB ____________________

A PLACE ____________________

CELEBRITY ____________________

ANIMAL ____________________

NUMBER ____________________

ADJECTIVE ____________________

LAST NAME ____________________

NOUN ____________________

TYPE OF FOOD ____________________

PERSON IN ROOM ____________________

FIRST NAME (MALE) ____________________

VERB ENDING IN "ING" ____________________

EXCLAMATION ____________________

VERB ____________________

MAD LIBS®

ONE MORE GAME

Convincing your __________ (NOUN) to let you stay up past your bedtime to play video games can be __________ (ADJECTIVE), but it's not impossible. Here are some __________ (ADJECTIVE) excuses to use when you need one last game.

- My __________ (PART OF THE BODY) hurts. The only way it'll feel better is if I __________ (VERB) these cyborgs and save (the) __________ (A PLACE).
- __________ (CELEBRITY) also plays __________ (ANIMAL) Hut so if you want me to be successful in life, please give me __________ (NUMBER) minutes to finish the __________ (ADJECTIVE) level.
- Mrs. __________ (LAST NAME), my __________ (NOUN) teacher, said that video games make you smart. She plays __________ (TYPE OF FOOD) *Assault*, so she knows.
- There's nothing else to do! __________ (PERSON IN ROOM) isn't here to play with, Grandpa __________ (FIRST NAME (MALE)) went to bed, and it's __________ (VERB ENDING IN "ING") outside.
- __________ (EXCLAMATION)! If you let me play *Night* __________ (VERB), I'll clean my room. Think about it.

MAD LIBS® is fun to play with friends, but you can also play it by yourself! To begin with, DO NOT look at the story on the page below. Fill in the blanks on this page with the words called for. Then, using the words you have selected, fill in the blank spaces in the story.

Now you've created your own hilarious MAD LIBS® game!

USE YOUR BRAIN

NOUN ________________

ADJECTIVE ________________

ANIMAL ________________

ADJECTIVE ________________

VERB ________________

PART OF THE BODY ________________

VERB ENDING IN "ING" ________________

CITY ________________

NOUN ________________

NOUN ________________

NUMBER ________________

PLURAL NOUN ________________

CELEBRITY ________________

ADJECTIVE ________________

PLURAL NOUN ________________

TYPE OF FOOD (PLURAL) ________________

NOUN ________________

MAD LIBS®

USE YOUR BRAIN

A/An ______________ is a terrible thing to waste. These games will keep
NOUN

your brain ______________!
ADJECTIVE

Poke the Pig: This little ____________ may not look ____________,
ANIMAL ADJECTIVE

but looks can be deceiving. See if you can ______________ it on its
VERB

______________ as many times as possible. Remember, time is
PART OF THE BODY

_____________________ out!
VERB ENDING IN "ING"

Trash Can City: Welcome to ______________, the dirtiest place around.
CITY

It's your job to pick up every ______________ and put it in the
NOUN

______________ before time runs out. You have ____________ minutes
NOUN NUMBER

to complete the task. Watch out for _________________ that stand in
PLURAL NOUN

your way.

Meals For Math: Are you the _______________ of the math world?
CELEBRITY

You'll need to be in order to complete this ______________ challenge.
ADJECTIVE

Collect a variety of _________________ and _______________________
PLURAL NOUN TYPE OF FOOD (PLURAL)

and count them all up before the ______________ rings.
NOUN

MAD LIBS® is fun to play with friends, but you can also play it by yourself! To begin with, DO NOT look at the story on the page below. Fill in the blanks on this page with the words called for. Then, using the words you have selected, fill in the blank spaces in the story.

Now you've created your own hilarious MAD LIBS® game!

WELCOME TO THE FUTURE

NUMBER ____________________

ADJECTIVE ____________________

A PLACE ____________________

ADJECTIVE ____________________

ANIMAL (PLURAL) ____________________

ADJECTIVE ____________________

PLURAL NOUN ____________________

VERB ____________________

NOUN ____________________

A PLACE ____________________

PERSON IN ROOM ____________________

TYPE OF FOOD ____________________

PLURAL NOUN ____________________

A PLACE ____________________

ANIMAL ____________________

VERB ____________________

PLURAL NOUN ____________________

MAD LIBS®

WELCOME TO THE FUTURE

It's the year ____________ (NUMBER) and life is hard. A group of ____________ (ADJECTIVE) robots have taken control of (the) ____________ (A PLACE). They're using their magic weapons to turn ____________ (ADJECTIVE) human beings into ____________ (ANIMAL (PLURAL)). Things are bad. There are ____________ (ADJECTIVE) ____________ (PLURAL NOUN) oozing out of the streets. It isn't safe anymore. You used to be able to ____________ (VERB) outside, but not anymore. A/An ____________ (NOUN) could see you and throw you in the ____________ (A PLACE) jail. I spoke to ____________ (PERSON IN ROOM) about getting more ____________ (TYPE OF FOOD). The stash that we have tastes like rotten ____________ (PLURAL NOUN). We're hiding out in (the) ____________ (A PLACE) now, but who knows what will happen next? A group of angry ____________ (ANIMAL)-Men could strike at any time. Maybe we should ____________ (VERB) once and for all. Maybe it's time to raise our ____________ (PLURAL NOUN) in the air and fight for what's right. That's what heroes would do.

MAD LIBS® is fun to play with friends, but you can also play it by yourself! To begin with, DO NOT look at the story on the page below. Fill in the blanks on this page with the words called for. Then, using the words you have selected, fill in the blank spaces in the story.

Now you've created your own hilarious MAD LIBS® game!

SMASH IT!

VERB ENDING IN "ING" ________________

ANIMAL ________________

COLOR ________________

NOUN ________________

ADJECTIVE ________________

PLURAL NOUN ________________

ADJECTIVE ________________

COLOR ________________

VERB ________________

ADJECTIVE ________________

ANIMAL ________________

ANIMAL ________________

VERB ENDING IN "ING" ________________

VERB ________________

ADVERB ________________

VERB ________________

ADVERB ________________

MAD LIBS

SMASH IT!

It's time for a battle royal. Who's ____________ (VERB ENDING IN "ING") today? Let's see what these brawlers can do.

Pikachu is a Pokémon that resembles a/an ____________ (ANIMAL) and can shoot bolts of electricity from the ____________ (COLOR) dots on his cheeks. Protecting his ____________ (NOUN) is not one of his strong suits.

Wario can be ____________ (ADJECTIVE) and gross during battle. He's been known to produce stinky ____________ (PLURAL NOUN) during a fight. Beware of his ____________ (ADJECTIVE) strength and his love of ____________ (COLOR) coins.

Snake can ____________ (VERB) very well and is a/an ____________ (ADJECTIVE) tactician. He's also quick like a/an ____________ (ANIMAL).

Duck Hunt combines the mischievousness of a/an ____________ (ANIMAL) with the ____________ (VERB ENDING IN "ING") skills of a duck. Together they ____________ (VERB) their enemies ____________ (ADVERB).

Pac-Man is superfast and can ____________ (VERB) ____________ (ADVERB). And he does it all with a smile.

MAD LIBS® is fun to play with friends, but you can also play it by yourself! To begin with, DO NOT look at the story on the page below. Fill in the blanks on this page with the words called for. Then, using the words you have selected, fill in the blank spaces in the story.

Now you've created your own hilarious MAD LIBS® game!

BATTLE BUDS

NOUN ________________

VERB ________________

ADJECTIVE ________________

NOUN ________________

NOUN ________________

ANIMAL (PLURAL) ________________

NOUN ________________

ADJECTIVE ________________

ADJECTIVE ________________

NOUN ________________

NOUN ________________

ADJECTIVE ________________

NOUN ________________

NUMBER ________________

PERSON IN ROOM ________________

TYPE OF FOOD ________________

TYPE OF LIQUID ________________

MAD LIBS®

BATTLE BUDS

Welcome to mindscape. Players, are you ready?

Kevin: Dude, are you ready for me to destroy your ____________ (NOUN)?

Colin: Ha-ha. You can't ____________ (VERB) anything with that ____________ (ADJECTIVE) ____________ (NOUN) of yours. It can barely function. You need a real ____________ (NOUN). Then you'll be able to use maximum power.

Kevin: Look out! A group of ____________ (ANIMAL (PLURAL)) are right behind you. Blast them with your ____________ (NOUN)!

Colin: That's too ____________ (ADJECTIVE). I need something a little more ____________ (ADJECTIVE) like a/an ____________ (NOUN).

Kevin: Whatever. Did you do your ____________ (NOUN) homework? It was pretty ____________ (ADJECTIVE).

Colin: Not yet. Hey, can I buy a magic ____________ (NOUN) from you? I've got ____________ (NUMBER) credits.

Kevin: Hold on. ____________ (PERSON IN ROOM) is calling me. I think its dinnertime. We're having ____________ (TYPE OF FOOD).

Colin: That's cool. I just spilled ____________ (TYPE OF LIQUID) all over my keyboard anyway. Till next time, buddy!

MAD LIBS® is fun to play with friends, but you can also play it by yourself! To begin with, DO NOT look at the story on the page below. Fill in the blanks on this page with the words called for. Then, using the words you have selected, fill in the blank spaces in the story.

Now you've created your own hilarious MAD LIBS® game!

MEGA QUIZ

OCCUPATION ____________

NOUN ____________

VERB ENDING IN "ING" ____________

ANIMAL ____________

VERB ____________

ADJECTIVE ____________

OCCUPATION ____________

NOUN ____________

ADJECTIVE ____________

NOUN ____________

VERB ENDING IN "ING" ____________

MAD LIBS

MEGA QUIZ

How well do you know Mega Man and his villains? Take this quiz and see!

1. Who is the brilliant ____________ (OCCUPATION) who uses his evil ____________ (NOUN) to create robots bent on ____________ (VERB ENDING IN "ING") Mega Man?

A. Professor Evil   C. Dr. Wily

B. Wicked Willy   D. Professor Man

2. Who uses his search ____________ (ANIMAL) to ____________ (VERB) up walls?

A. Slither   C. The Fox

B. Snake Man   D. Birdman

3. This villain is a/an ____________ (ADJECTIVE) ____________ (OCCUPATION) who uses a sharp ____________ (NOUN) to pierce ____________ (ADJECTIVE) surfaces.

A. Tomahawk Man   C. Clown Man

B. Splash Woman   D. Zebular

4. This bad guy has a/an ____________ (NOUN) on his head and loves ____________ (VERB ENDING IN "ING"). He's a bit of a daredevil.

A. Star Man   C. Bomb Man

B. Wily Capsule   D. Stone Man

MAD LIBS® is fun to play with friends, but you can also play it by yourself! To begin with, DO NOT look at the story on the page below. Fill in the blanks on this page with the words called for. Then, using the words you have selected, fill in the blank spaces in the story.

Now you've created your own hilarious MAD LIBS® game!

LET'S DRIVE: MYRTLE BEACH

ADJECTIVE ____________________

PLURAL NOUN ____________________

PLURAL NOUN ____________________

ADJECTIVE ____________________

VEHICLE ____________________

TYPE OF FOOD ____________________

ANIMAL (PLURAL) ____________________

PART OF THE BODY (PLURAL) ____________________

NOUN ____________________

SILLY WORD ____________________

NOUN ____________________

NOUN ____________________

VERB ____________________

NOUN ____________________

ADJECTIVE ____________________

MAD LIBS
LET'S DRIVE: MYRTLE BEACH

Welcome to the Grand Strand—where the people are hot and the cars are ____________ (ADJECTIVE).

But ____________ (PLURAL NOUN) can be deceiving. There's sun, ____________ (PLURAL NOUN), and a/an ____________ (ADJECTIVE) ocean, but that doesn't mean crime takes a vacation. Gas up your ____________ (VEHICLE) and head down to the boulevard for some ____________ (TYPE OF FOOD). But be careful, there are ____________ (ANIMAL (PLURAL)) everywhere waiting to strike. Take a good look around. Use your ____________ (PART OF THE BODY (PLURAL)). It's up to you to figure out who's a friend and who's a/an ____________ (NOUN). Once you meet Doctor ____________ (SILLY WORD), he'll tell you where to find the ____________ (NOUN). Just remember, don't trust anyone, not even your own ____________ (NOUN). People are waiting to ____________ (VERB) you all over this city. Some people say life's a/an ____________ (NOUN). Well, they've never been to ____________ (ADJECTIVE) Beach.

MAD LIBS® is fun to play with friends, but you can also play it by yourself! To begin with, DO NOT look at the story on the page below. Fill in the blanks on this page with the words called for. Then, using the words you have selected, fill in the blank spaces in the story.

Now you've created your own hilarious MAD LIBS® game!

WORK IT OUT!

VERB ENDING IN "ING" ________________

VERB ________________

PART OF THE BODY ________________

ADJECTIVE ________________

NUMBER ________________

NOUN ________________

ADJECTIVE ________________

PART OF THE BODY ________________

VERB ________________

NOUN ________________

PART OF THE BODY ________________

VERB ________________

ANIMAL ________________

ADJECTIVE ________________

VERB ________________

NUMBER ________________

PART OF THE BODY ________________

NOUN ________________

MAD LIBS

WORK IT OUT!

There's no ____________ (VERB ENDING IN "ING") in *Workout World*. There's only working out! Set your controls to fun and get ready to ____________ (VERB).

Wind grasp: Use your ____________ (PART OF THE BODY) to grab as much wind as possible and put it into your ____________ (ADJECTIVE) pouch. Once you have ____________ (NUMBER) pouches filled, dump them out and start over.

Exercise penny: Bend down and place a/an ____________ (NOUN) on the ground in front of you. Stare at it until you feel ____________ (ADJECTIVE). Repeat as needed.

Wiggle worm: Take your ____________ (PART OF THE BODY) and ____________ (VERB) it like it's a hot ____________ (NOUN). Then take your other ____________ (PART OF THE BODY) and ____________ (VERB) it like it's a/an ____________ (ANIMAL). Congratulations. You're a wiggle worm.

Sittin' mat: Get out your ____________ (ADJECTIVE) mat and ____________ (VERB) on it for ____________ (NUMBER) minutes. This will allow your ____________ (PART OF THE BODY) to relax. Feel the ____________ (NOUN) move through you.

MAD LIBS® is fun to play with friends, but you can also play it by yourself! To begin with, DO NOT look at the story on the page below. Fill in the blanks on this page with the words called for. Then, using the words you have selected, fill in the blank spaces in the story.

Now you've created your own hilarious MAD LIBS® game!

ZOMBIE INVASION

SILLY WORD ____________________

NOUN ____________________

NOUN ____________________

ADJECTIVE ____________________

ADJECTIVE ____________________

PLURAL NOUN ____________________

TYPE OF FOOD (PLURAL) ____________________

VERB ____________________

ANIMAL ____________________

CELEBRITY (MALE) ____________________

EXCLAMATION ____________________

PLURAL NOUN ____________________

ADJECTIVE ____________________

SILLY WORD ____________________

NOUN ____________________

A PLACE ____________________

NOUN ____________________

FIRST NAME (MALE) ____________________

MAD LIBS®

ZOMBIE INVASION

Dear Aunt ____________ (SILLY WORD),

I hope this ____________ (NOUN) gets to you. I might be the last person on Planet ____________ (NOUN). It's really ____________ (ADJECTIVE) here because of all the zombies. They aren't like the ____________ (ADJECTIVE) zombies we used to watch on TV. They actually eat ____________ (PLURAL NOUN) and ____________ (TYPE OF FOOD (PLURAL))! I saw one of them ____________ (VERB) a/an ____________ (ANIMAL) the other day. It was more mean than scary. Sometimes I think, "What would ____________ (CELEBRITY (MALE)) do in my situation?" I think he would say, "____________ (EXCLAMATION)! It's time to get out our ____________ (PLURAL NOUN) and save the world!" Anyway, I hope this letter isn't too ____________ (ADJECTIVE). Please tell Uncle ____________ (SILLY WORD) that I say hello. Are you going anywhere this ____________ (NOUN)? I'd go to (the) ____________ (A PLACE), but I think there might be too many zombies there. Have a good ____________ (NOUN)!

Love,

____________ (FIRST NAME (MALE))

MAD LIBS® is fun to play with friends, but you can also play it by yourself! To begin with, DO NOT look at the story on the page below. Fill in the blanks on this page with the words called for. Then, using the words you have selected, fill in the blank spaces in the story.

Now you've created your own hilarious MAD LIBS® game!

LET'S FIGHT!

NOUN ____________

PART OF THE BODY (PLURAL) ____________

VERB ____________

ADJECTIVE ____________

OCCUPATION ____________

VERB ENDING IN "ING" ____________

VERB ____________

PLURAL NOUN ____________

PLURAL NOUN ____________

PART OF THE BODY (PLURAL) ____________

ANIMAL ____________

ADJECTIVE ____________

SILLY WORD ____________

ADJECTIVE ____________

A PLACE ____________

TYPE OF FOOD ____________

VERB ENDING IN "ING" ____________

PART OF THE BODY (PLURAL) ____________

MAD LIBS®

LET'S FIGHT!

They're the best at what they do, and what they do is fight! They are the awesome stars of ____________ (NOUN) *Fighter*.

Ryu: He may not use his ____________ (PART OF THE BODY (PLURAL)) very much, but his fists ____________ (VERB) for him. Ryu is a/an ____________ (ADJECTIVE) student who is serious about becoming a master ____________ (OCCUPATION). He's always ____________ (VERB ENDING IN "ING") his enemy, waiting for the right time to ____________ (VERB).

Cammy: Cammy keeps her ____________ (PLURAL NOUN) close and her ____________ (PLURAL NOUN) closer. Don't let her kind ____________ (PART OF THE BODY (PLURAL)) fool you—she also goes by the nickname Killer ____________ (ANIMAL).

Bison: There is no one more ____________ (ADJECTIVE) than Bison. He craves power. A country like ____________ (SILLY WORD) will never be enough for him. He won't stop until he's the most ____________ (ADJECTIVE) martial artist in the entire ____________ (A PLACE).

Chun-Li: When it comes to superfast reflexes, Chun-Li takes the ____________ (TYPE OF FOOD). Her kick sends her enemies ____________ (VERB ENDING IN "ING") to the ground on their ____________ (PART OF THE BODY (PLURAL)).

MAD LIBS® is fun to play with friends, but you can also play it by yourself! To begin with, DO NOT look at the story on the page below. Fill in the blanks on this page with the words called for. Then, using the words you have selected, fill in the blank spaces in the story.

Now you've created your own hilarious MAD LIBS® game!

GOOD-BYE FOREVER

FIRST NAME ________________

A PLACE ________________

ADJECTIVE ________________

PERSON IN ROOM ________________

TYPE OF FOOD ________________

NOUN ________________

ADJECTIVE ________________

ANIMAL ________________

ADJECTIVE ________________

PLURAL NOUN ________________

PART OF THE BODY (PLURAL) ________________

PERSON IN ROOM ________________

A PLACE ________________

CELEBRITY ________________

PLURAL NOUN ________________

FIRST NAME ________________

MAD LIBS®

GOOD-BYE FOREVER

Dear _______________ (FIRST NAME),

I'm sorry to tell you this, but I'm leaving you. Every day I come home from (the) _______________ (A PLACE) and you're playing _______________ (ADJECTIVE) *Fortress* with _______________ (PERSON IN ROOM). What about our time together? You said you would take me out for _______________ (TYPE OF FOOD) on _______________ (NOUN) Day, but you never did. You said you would take me to see *The* _______________ (ADJECTIVE) _______________ (ANIMAL) *of Mr. Marlow,* but you never did. It's my _______________ (ADJECTIVE) movie! All you want to do is shoot _______________ (PLURAL NOUN) at people's _______________ (PART OF THE BODY (PLURAL)) on the computer. It's ruining my life. Even _______________ (PERSON IN ROOM) said that you play too much! When are we going to (the) _______________ (A PLACE)? When are you introducing me to _______________ (CELEBRITY)? I guess those were all lies. Thanks for the _______________ (PLURAL NOUN) but it's over. Good-bye forever.

Sincerely,

_______________ (FIRST NAME)

MAD LIBS® is fun to play with friends, but you can also play it by yourself! To begin with, DO NOT look at the story on the page below. Fill in the blanks on this page with the words called for. Then, using the words you have selected, fill in the blank spaces in the story.

Now you've created your own hilarious MAD LIBS® game!

ROBOT VAMPIRE NINJA PIRATE & FRIENDS

NOUN ____________________

ANIMAL (PLURAL) ____________________

NOUN ____________________

ADJECTIVE ____________________

A PLACE ____________________

TYPE OF LIQUID ____________________

NOUN ____________________

NOUN ____________________

TYPE OF FOOD ____________________

NOUN ____________________

ADJECTIVE ____________________

ADJECTIVE ____________________

VERB ____________________

PERSON IN ROOM ____________________

ADJECTIVE ____________________

MAD LIBS

ROBOT VAMPIRE NINJA PIRATE & FRIENDS

Are you looking for a/an ____________ (NOUN) that gives you action, excitement, and an army of cloned ____________ (ANIMAL (PLURAL))? Look no further! This game has everything. A wicked ____________ (NOUN) Queen cast a/an ____________ (ADJECTIVE) spell that turned everyone in (the) ____________ (A PLACE) into ____________ (TYPE OF LIQUID). Now it's up to Robot Vampire Ninja Pirate and his friends to save the ____________ (NOUN). It won't be easy though. This isn't ____________ (NOUN)-ball. It's a good thing they brought ____________ (TYPE OF FOOD), because they're going to need it. Will ____________ (NOUN) Man and ____________ (ADJECTIVE) Lady use their powers to reverse the spell? Or maybe Robot Vampire Ninja Pirate will use his ____________ (ADJECTIVE) blaster to ____________ (VERB) the Queen and end her reign of terror? It's all up to ____________ (PERSON IN ROOM). Log on today for your free ____________ (ADJECTIVE) codes and join the battle!

MAD LIBS® is fun to play with friends, but you can also play it by yourself! To begin with, DO NOT look at the story on the page below. Fill in the blanks on this page with the words called for. Then, using the words you have selected, fill in the blank spaces in the story.

Now you've created your own hilarious MAD LIBS® game!

THE EXCELLENT ANTONIO TRIPLETS

VEHICLE ______________________

ADJECTIVE ______________________

A PLACE ______________________

VERB ______________________

PLURAL NOUN ______________________

PART OF THE BODY (PLURAL) ______________________

VERB ______________________

ADJECTIVE ______________________

PART OF THE BODY (PLURAL) ______________________

NOUN ______________________

ADJECTIVE ______________________

ANIMAL ______________________

TYPE OF LIQUID ______________________

NOUN ______________________

VERB ENDING IN "ING" ______________________

ADJECTIVE ______________________

ADJECTIVE ______________________

OCCUPATION ______________________

MAD LIBS®

THE EXCELLENT ANTONIO TRIPLETS

Alfonso: Prince Grape has been kidnapped! Time to hop in the

____________ and go to ____________ City.
VEHICLE ADJECTIVE

Giovanni: No, Alfonso! We are electricians from (the) ____________.
A PLACE

We are not some kind of heroes.

Sal: We are triplets who ____________ when duty calls! If the Brussels
VERB

Sprout Kingdom needs us then we will strap ____________ on our
PLURAL NOUN

____________ and do the job.
PART OF THE BODY (PLURAL)

Giovanni: But the Salamander Queen can ____________! She has
VERB

____________ ____________. What can we do? Throw
ADJECTIVE PART OF THE BODY (PLURAL)

a/an ____________ at her?
NOUN

Alfonso: Brother, we must be like the ____________ ____________.
ADJECTIVE ANIMAL

We'll sneak up on her with our ____________ guns and then,
TYPE OF LIQUID

when she is resting on her ____________, we will strike!
NOUN

Sal: Personally, I look forward to ____________ her
VERB ENDING IN "ING"

____________ minions. Let us do it for Prince Grape.
ADJECTIVE

Giovanni: You both make very ____________ points. It's time to be
ADJECTIVE

a/an ____________. For Prince Grape!
OCCUPATION

MAD LIBS® is fun to play with friends, but you can also play it by yourself! To begin with, DO NOT look at the story on the page below. Fill in the blanks on this page with the words called for. Then, using the words you have selected, fill in the blank spaces in the story.

Now you've created your own hilarious MAD LIBS® game!

CONVENTION TIME!

NOUN ______________________

ADJECTIVE ______________________

NOUN ______________________

TYPE OF FOOD (PLURAL) ______________________

NUMBER ______________________

PERSON IN ROOM ______________________

NOUN ______________________

A PLACE ______________________

ARTICLE OF CLOTHING ______________________

NOUN ______________________

VERB ______________________

ADJECTIVE ______________________

NOUN ______________________

PERSON IN ROOM ______________________

PLURAL NOUN ______________________

NOUN ______________________

MAD LIBS®

CONVENTION TIME!

Welcome to Gamer Con 5000! We're excited to have you. Please check your __________ (NOUN) for a list of __________ (ADJECTIVE) items you may bring inside the __________ (NOUN). __________ (TYPE OF FOOD (PLURAL)) are strictly prohibited! Gaming Centers will be set up in __________ (NUMBER) locations, and attendees will be divided up by character. If you are dressed as __________ (PERSON IN ROOM) from __________ (NOUN), please check in at (the) __________ (A PLACE). If you are wearing a/an __________ (ARTICLE OF CLOTHING), you will be denied entry unless accompanied by your __________ (NOUN). Attendees looking to play *Star* __________ (VERB) and *The* __________ (ADJECTIVE) __________ (NOUN) should register online. No one dressed as __________ (PERSON IN ROOM) will be allowed in the bathrooms for any reason. Please bring extra __________ (PLURAL NOUN) and remember to have a/an __________ (NOUN)!